You Are
Worthless

You Are Worthless

Depressing Nuggets of Wisdom Sure to Ruin Your Day

Dr. Oswald T. Pratt
& Dr. Scott Dikkers

**Andrews McMeel
Publishing**

Kansas City

www.andrewsmcmeel.com

99 00 01 02 03 RDC 10 9 8 7 6 5 4 3 2 1

Library of Congress Cataloging-in-Publication Data
Pratt, Oswald, T.
    You are worthless : depressing nuggets of wisdom sure to ruin your day / Oswald T. Pratt & Scott Dikkers.
        p.   cm.
    ISBN 0-7407-0025-1 (pbk.)
    1. Self-actualization (Psychology) Humor.   2. Depression, Mental Humor.   3. Self-esteem Humor.   I. Dikkers, Scott.   II. Title.
PN6231.P785P73 1999
818'.5402—dc21   99-22170
                                                                    CIP

Book design by Holly Camerlinck

This book is a parody, and is not intended to be construed as actual advice.

——— *Attention: Schools and Businesses* ———

Andrews McMeel books are available at quantity discounts with bulk purchase for educational, business, or sales promotional use. For information, please write to: Special Sales Department, Andrews McMeel Publishing, 4520 Main Street, Kansas City, Missouri 64111.

Contents

You Are Worthless

Introduction

I'm a terrible psychologist. Nobody likes me. Nobody listens to me. I wish I could just quit.

Sometimes, when I tell people that I want to quit dispensing self-help advice, they point to the fact that I've had a successful practice in the Fresno, California, area for over seven years and have written four best-selling books. You call that success? The books aren't that good, and the practice is only doing well because the other people I work with are pulling most of the weight. I'm just a worthless bum, really. I can't do anything right. I don't even know why I try.

The main thing is, none of my patients ever seem to get better. I don't know what I'm doing wrong; I'm only being honest with them about their lives. I tell them what I think—you know, give them my professional opinion—and they just fall apart. It's really kind of depressing. Maybe the problem is that most of them are such complete losers. I really hate them, to be honest with you.

I treated this guy once who got fired from his job and was dumped by his wife in the same week! Talk about rough. He was sobbing like an infant when he came into my office. He said I was his last hope, that he just needed one little ray of hope to cling to. I told him that there was no hope, that his wife obviously realized how unappealing and unattractive and stupid he is, and had to move on to someone better—someone who really had something to offer a woman. I also told him that his boss probably figured out how much of a fraud he was at work, that he was pretty much draining money out of the company payroll for keeping a chair warm. He just kept on crying. Boy, I sure did feel unappreciated. I'm, like, "Why did you even come in here if you're not interested in what I have to tell you? I'm just telling it like it is. The truth hurts, buddy." Anyway, I said I didn't really need to be listening to his sob story and told him to take a hike.

It's really a tough job, having to listen to pathetic people whining all the time. I wish I could quit. But what else am I going to do? I'm too old to start over. God, I hate myself.

Well, whatever your sorry-ass problem is, I hope the nuggets of wisdom in this book help. Aw, who am I kidding? This book isn't going to help anybody. Nothing I do ever amounts to anything.

Dr. Oswald T. Pratt

Your Worthless Self

You are worthless.

You don't have any outstanding qualities. It's safe to say that you're pretty much just like everybody else.

Really. What good are you? Name three attributes that set you apart from others.

Ah, to hell with you.

If you take a big risk and follow your dream, chances are you're going to fall flat on your face. On the upside, everyone around you will get a good laugh.

You should find a role model who's been very successful in a vocation that you aspire to, or someone famous that you can look up to. Now, imagine what that person would say upon meeting you: "Yeah, great, now get lost. Security!"

Try another role-model exercise: Picture someone you look up to who is very rich, good-looking, successful, and loved by everyone. Now slowly count to one million, because that's how many years in which you will never be as rich, good-looking, successful, or loved as that person.

"For all the good it'll do ya, I welcome all you losers to use me as a role model."

You often say that you're not doing exactly what you want to be doing with your life. You will continue saying this until you die.

You're not living up to your full potential.
You never will.

You are good for nothing.

*I would be willing to wager that
at some point your mother was
holding you, looking at you, saying
to herself, "What was I thinking?"*

"maybe this was a huge mistake."

Tomorrow is going to be even worse than today.

Think for a moment about just how bad things
have been going lately.

You're really up shit creek.

I sure wouldn't want to be in your shoes.

Geez, your life really sucks.

I hate to see someone cry. So, get lost, would you?

Maybe you should binge on ice cream.

✀

Mask the pain with drugs.

Just so you know, there's nothing anyone can do to make things any better.

Nobody's really interested in making things better for you anyway.

You're going to feel terrible for a long, long time.

You'll probably never get over these hard times.

You sound like a big baby with all your sobbing and blubbering.

"My life is horrible!"

I don't like you.

You're not a very pleasant person to be around.

You're boring.

When you talk, people are only pretending to be interested. Trust me on this. Their head is somewhere else.

Come to grips with your problems by having
a complete emotional breakdown.

Beat yourself up a little today.

Have you considered suicide?

Killing yourself would be a good idea. The only
problem is that you don't have the guts.

You can buy all the soaps, perfumes
and deodorants you want. But rest assured,
your body will still emit several
very unpleasant odors.

You probably don't know when the Civil War
was fought.

You've spent more time watching
America's Funniest Home Videos than you've
spent reading Beckett. That, I'm afraid,
is a fact.

As you get older, you are going to have less and less control over your bladder.

❧

You're fat.

❧

When they perform an autopsy on you, they're going to have to peel away several inches of viscous, yellow fat to get a look at your vital organs.

❧

You think you're a lot smarter than a chimpanzee. But let's turn back time and raise you in the wild with chimpanzees for parents. Not too smart now, are you, chimpanzee-man?

*If you fell off a horse and were
paralyzed from the neck down
like Christopher Reeve, you wouldn't be
the noble, I'm-going-to-beat-this-thing
hero like they make him out to be.
You'd spend every waking moment sobbing
and wishing you were dead. In fact,
that's probably what he's doing
right now.*

"If only I'd been killed."

In the face of dire adversity, you would crumble.

You've probably said something like
"What's this world coming to?" Well, look
around, it's come to quite a sad state of affairs:
us listening to you whining.

Boy, you're really screwed up.

You're going to die someday.
It's probably going to hurt.

You're not that good-looking.

When people stand really close to you
and can examine your skin,
they're thinking, "Gross."

The law of averages would suggest
that at some point in your life,
someone has referred to you
as "that idiot."

The last time someone complimented you
by saying that you were
a really sweet person, you knew,
deep down, that it wasn't true.

When was the last time
you did something you were proud of?
Keep thinking. I bet
you're stumped.

*Eight things
you can do
to feel worthless
today*

*Call a relative and tell him or her
you're going to change your life around.
Let the condescending cry of "Ha!"
echo in your mind.*

*G*o on one of Richard Simmons' infomercials and let him tell you that you're not really all that pathetic.

*Draw something. Make it
as beautiful as you can. When you're
done, look at it and realize
just how bad you are at drawing.*

Fall and break your collarbone.
Blame your own clumsiness.

*Reveal to a dear friend
that your life is falling apart
and watch her quickly lose interest
and distance herself from you.*

*Storm your local fast-food joint
with a gun, then be stunned by the
realization that you don't have the guts
to shoot anybody. Get arrested and
spend several years in prison anyway.*

Go for a drive and make a lot of sudden lane changes and incorrect turn signals. Listen very carefully to the things the other drivers yell at you.

Wear something that makes your
ass look big.

Maybe it would feel good to hurt someone.

You will die lonely.

*You are really messed up. Yes, it's true
that everybody is messed up
to a certain extent. But you are a lot more
messed up than other people.*

You don't have what it takes.

You are a loser.

You do not have the right to feel the way you are feeling right now.

It's not okay.

When people reflect on the world and say,
"There're so many stupid people
in the world,"
they're talking about you.

You know, everybody's pretty sick and tired of
hearing about all your problems.

Your
Good-For-
Nothing
Friends

Your friends say they like you, but really they only like how they feel around you. You barely figure into the equation at all.

Sometimes your friends hang out with you not because they enjoy your company, but because they feel sorry for you. If they have to keep doing this much longer, they're going to dump you like a hot potato.

*Another reason your friends
may call you is in order to unload
a bunch of their sob stories on you.
Do you really need that?*

"Please come over and
try to cheer me up...
um, no, there's
nothing in it for you."

If you had never met your friends,
and you had been born in Iraq or something,
they would probably not care if you got bombed.
In fact, they might support the idea.

You know those beer commercials where all those
really good friends are getting together to drink
and they're all super good-looking and seem to be
incredibly close? Fess up, you don't have any
friends like that.

In a pinch, can you really count on your friends?

When the chips are down, your friends are just going to save their own hides. I guarantee it.

Your friends are probably out to get you.

Screw them!

Your friends
only hang out with you
because they want something
from you.

"could I borrow some shit?"

Your friends are just a bunch of parasites.

What do you really get from your friends?
Most of them are just like you, anyway.
And that seems like a pretty boring setup.

There are a lot of things you could admit
to your friends that would cause them
to never call you again.

*If they knew who you really were,
they'd hate you.*

Keep up the charade.

*Keep smiling and laughing.
They'll never suspect.*

*Let's sit down and actually count the genuine,
true friends you have. It's not that many, is it?*

*Actually, you probably don't have
a single friend.*

Oh, except Jesus. He's your friend.
Why don't you call him and see if he
wants to hang out?

If you do have any friends, most likely
they just don't know you well enough yet.
Once they get to know you and figure out
how much of a basket case you are,
they'll be gone like a shot.

The reverse is also true.
Your friends are a bunch of pathetic losers,
and you should not waste
your time with them.

Think about all the times your friends have
crossed you. Let that feeling stew.

*Be sure never to tell your friends
you love them. This is awkward,
and best avoided.*

Your friends don't really like you for who you are.

A true friend is a gift from God. Since God doesn't exist, guess what? Neither do true friends.

How to identify a true friend

They exist only in your dreams.

You are paying them
to act like one, such as
a therapist, masseuse, or whore.

They smile at you from the television.

They come in a syringe.

They are one hundred—proof.

Wouldn't it be great
if all those ingrates
who call themselves your friends
would just leave you the hell alone?

You don't need your friends.

Look at that photo you have
of you and your best friend—you know,
the one where you have your arms
around each other and are smiling
and looking right at the camera.
You may think back fondly to that
moment, but, if you'll recall, you were
both asked to fake that smile.

*Your friends care a lot more about themselves
than they do about you.*

*If you have any faith in your friends,
question it. Question it hard.*

All The Other Idiots

People are basically evil.

People are really only looking out for
themselves.

It's only the thin veneer of law and order
that keeps us all from looting grocery stores
and running through the streets
setting fire to police cars.
(When the riots begin, try to make off with one
of those four-head VCRs.)

Why should you lift a finger to help anybody?
They're all a bunch of idiots.

Nobody likes you.

At the end of the day, who's really there
for you? Who really cares?
Nobody.

What has anyone ever done for you?
To hell with them.

Nobody gives a damn about you.

People will stab you in the back if given
half the chance.

If they were paid a half a million dollars
and were guaranteed to get off scot-free,
most people would have no problem killing you.
They've done surveys on this.

If you were mugged and beaten on a busy street, 98 percent of your fellow citizens would stand by and watch. This is a statistically proven fact.

"p- please... help... me..."

When you're crossing the street,
people in cars are making jokes about
getting points for running you down.

Remember during the Oliver North hearings
in the 1980s when someone mentioned the
supersecret National Security Act in which
the Constitution of the United States would be
suspended in the event of a national emergency?
Anyway, Senator Inouye, I think it was,
said that it was a sensitive matter
and should not be discussed on TV, and
it was quickly dropped. That's too bad, because
I was kind of interested in hearing about that.
They're all trying to screw us over.
You know they are.

Most people are terrible at their jobs.

Nobody has any idea what they're doing.

*Next time you fly on an airplane,
think of the airplane technician
who probably neglected to tighten a vital
fuselage bolt because he all of a sudden needed
to go buy a candy bar, or had to call his
girlfriend, or just shrugged his shoulders and
decided not to tighten it because he was mad
at his boss that day. Think of the hundreds
of thousands of such bolts on every airplane.
You're trusting your life to common dullards
like this all the time.*

Trust no one.

When you're really down and out, who do you
turn to, your fucked-up family?
Your no-account friends? Basically, you've
got no one. Except maybe your counselor.
And I'm only in it for the money,
I can assure you of that.

You know those local TV news reporters who tell you about all the day's events in your area? I suspect you sit alone in front of the TV and appreciate them because they always say they care about you, and about your community. Here's the sad truth: they hate you, and your community. I don't mean in some abstract sense, I mean they really hate you. They talk about you during the commercial break: "I couldn't care less about these stupid viewers," they say. "And fuck this jerkwater community. They can all rot in hell for all I care. I'm only playing this penny-ante game until I get a job with the network."

"I'll be back to play-act more concern after this...."

Ninety-five percent of the people on this planet live in painful, abject poverty. And you don't care. Heck, none of us do.

A person just died of starvation in the time it took for you to read that. Who gives a flying fart? He or she was probably clear across the other side of the world anyway.

The U.S. is only 5 percent of the world's population, but we consume 80 percent of its resources.

Our world is nothing but 95 percent poverty-stricken, bloated-stomached babies and 5 percent money-grubbing pricks. In your lifetime, you've only met people from the latter category.

The world is going to hell in a handbasket.

There are too many goddamned people on this planet.

Why do people keep having kids?

People who have kids are idiots.

"Let's add one more needless person to this doomed world!"

Your parents didn't think about what they were
doing for a second. They just reproduced like
dumb apes, and here you are—
part of the problem.

✑

Your parents didn't love you enough.

✑

Your family is messed up.

✑

Your family only tolerates you because you have
some of the same genetic material as them.
They're basically in it for themselves.

Your family is a bunch of wackos.

Those old ladies at the grocery store who hand
out free samples of pizza rolls are wiping their
asses with those things before they hand them out.

People are probably trying to poison you.

People who work in the food-service industry are probably spitting in the food a lot more often than you'd think.

"Here you are, sir. Have a real nice day now."

You are being watched.

There are people out to get you.

There are secret cameras everywhere.

It's a conspiracy.

When they try to give you pills, fight them with all your strength.

Maybe other people aren't what they seem at all. Maybe this is all an elaborate setup, and really you were abducted by aliens a long time ago and have been strapped to a table in an alien prison for years with needles stuck in your brain, and they're making you imagine your whole life as some kind of twisted experiment. Don't let them do it. Fuck with the experiment. Go shoot some people in a mall.

How do you know your best friend isn't one of them?

Police can't be trusted. They're all owned by the mob.

The clergy can't be trusted. All they ever do is rape little boys.

The bus driver would just as soon slit your throat as give you a ride.

At least you can count on
your elected officials.

"Vote for me — I'm the
one you can trust."

All the telemarketers and direct-mail bastards are trying to steal from you. And they will never leave you alone.

That guy behind the counter at the drugstore just wants to knock you down and rifle through your pockets for loose change.

The

Nightmare

That Is

Love

You will spend the rest of your life alone.

You have a lot of physical flaws. How do you expect anyone to be attracted to you?

Beyond mere attraction, how do you expect someone to actually fall in love with you? Why, the notion is preposterous.

If you're in a relationship right now, you should know that your special friend doesn't really love you; he or she is just using you.

Love is a deep, dark chasm of pain and loss.

No one will ever love you.

You have nothing to offer
a potential mate.

"Get away from me."

No one falls in love with a loser.
Get a clue.

When you fall in love, get married and embark upon a life together, enjoy those first three or four years, because that's how long it will last.

Love is simply a chemical response in the brain to physical stimuli indicating that a potential mate has been found. It is not special or magical.

You are not very good in bed.

The Nine Stages of Love:

1. Attraction
2. Infatuation
3. Surrender
4. Commitment
5. Malaise
6. Attraction to Others
7. Jealousy
8. Abandonment
9. Heartbreak

It's probably best that you never talk to your mate about sex.

Admit it, you're tired of having sex with the same person. Furthermore, that person isn't really all that sexy.

I give your current relationship two years, tops.

What is sex? You grope somebody while he or she gropes you, you spit in each other's mouth. You start grunting like dogs. There's probably one orgasm—a brief moment of sensory bliss, then you have to listen to this cow blab about his or her stupid, intimate thoughts. Frankly, I would much rather have gone to a good movie or had a big chocolate-chip cookie.

Have you considered a life of prostitution? As it is, you're just going through the motions when you have sex. You might as well be getting paid.

Somebody better than you is bound to come along and steal your loved one away.

What do you really have
to offer someone in a relationship?
Besides all your crying
and blubbering, I mean.

"You are so unattractive
right now."

Screaming and yelling will make you feel better, especially if you direct your anger at someone you care about.

No one will ever love you as much as your mother did. And her love for you completely fucked you up, let's face it.

Wow, your significant other could do so much better.

I know this real pathetic loser who would be great for you.

There's nothing very special about your special someone. Anyone would have sufficed.

"I guess you'll do."

The only reason you want someone to love you is for all the back rubs. And in the end, a professional masseuse would be cheaper. And a hell of a lot better. Think about it.

Your genitals are hideous.

What did you eat? I ask because your breath smells terrible.

Your various exes probably got over you pretty easily.

Your ass stinks.

You are plain looking.

You are not particularly special.

The next time you have sex, fixate on just how horribly unattractive your body is.

You should be ashamed of your body.

You are a little chunky.

*Why do
I love thee?
Let me count
the ways*

❣ *Because you've been the person who's been in closer proximity to me than anyone else lately.*

❣ *Because you remind me of my parents.*

❣ *Because my biological clock is ticking, and I ain't wasting any time.*

❣ *Because you asked me out once or twice.*

❣ *Because of the unfortunate lack of birth control that one time.*

❣ *Because you tolerate me.*

❣ *Because you didn't push me away when I first groped you.*

❣ *Because you let me have sex with you.*

You are better off alone.

You are no good for anybody.

Someday your special someone is going to wake up and realize that you're not worth the time of day, and he or she is going to leave you and never speak to you again.

You should get out of your relationship first, before your partner does. It hurts a lot less to dump someone than it does to get dumped.

Save your own skin.

Look out for number one.

Statistically speaking, there is a 65 percent chance that the love of your life is having an affair. Be very suspicious.

Your special someone is far less attracted to you than to someone he or she saw on television once.

When your relationship is over, you'll know it because that's when you'll decide to hang on to it and be miserable for three years more.

Why not try a personals ad? You'll probably find someone who seems magically suited to you. That's because everyone in the personals scene is just as lonely and pathetic as you are.

You can never really know the person you are in love with. He or she could turn on you any second.

No matter how much you think you love someone or trust someone, know this: Between you and everyone else on this planet there is a dark, infinite chasm that can never be crossed.

The inside of your special someone smells like a barn.

Love is a selfish, indulgent emotion.

Love feels like being stabbed in the back with an ice pick.

Love will hurt you.

Love hurts.

You know what really hurts? Love.

Here is something: Love hurts.

Do you know what love feels like? It hurts.

Love. It hurts like hell.

*Falling in love is like getting kicked
in the shins.*

*Love conquers all, rapes all, pillages all, and
leaves all for dead.*

Are you in love? Sucker.

When someone says, "I love you," what they really mean is, "I love the way I feel when anyone expresses an interest in me, in this case, you."

It is better to have loved and lost than to have hot needles slowly driven into your eyeballs.

Most American boys have 60 percent of their most sexually sensitive skin hacked off with a knife at birth without anesthetic.

Three out of four women are sexually abused
or assaulted in their lifetimes.

This thing we call civilization
is basically just a bunch of thugs
hoping to rape as many people as possible.

At the peak of orgasm, you probably
don't care who you're having sex with.

Women are uptight.

Men are jerks.

Most women hardly ever have orgasms.
Reason: They're too uptight.

Most men will never fully submit to a loving
relationship. Reason: They're jerks.

You know when you're brokenhearted and
pining for your lost love and sobbing
and blubbering all the time? Well,
you look pathetic when you're doing that.

Next time you get dumped, it might
comfort you to remember this: You will never
find a love like that ever again—that person
meant everything to you, and you will never
find anyone that special ever again.

During sex, you are an unattractive,
heaving mass that leaves its partner feeling
as though he or she has been attacked
by a walrus.

You are gross.

You have sexual tendencies that are
not normal, and you should be ashamed of them.

If you truly love someone, then you are the
biggest chump of all.

The
Goddamned
Kids

So, you're a parent! You ignorant dupe.

You were stupid to have kids. Hell, even your kids think so.

What have your children ever done for you? Was it really worth it to have them?

You have a lot of obligations because of your kids. Think about all those obligations for a moment and let them weigh you down.

Admit it, you resent those damned kids.

No one else in this society is particularly grateful to you for bringing those rotten kids into the world.

Why did you want to bring more people into this world? You know they're only going to end up miserable failures like you. You're mean.

People are stupid. This includes your kids.

You know, you just created a lot of work for everybody else when you decided to have kids.

You were having enough trouble just taking care of yourself. What were you thinking adding to your load?

"Dad? Dad? Dad? Dad? Dad? Dad? Dad? Dad? Dad? Dad? Dad? Dad?"

Oh, sure, they're cute when they're small. But when they get big, they're just as dumb and annoying as everybody else.

What is it about the genetic bond that makes you care about your kids? I'll tell you what it is: It's selfishness. You only care about yourself and your own precious genes. Well, let me tell you something, none of the rest of us give a crap.

Take your kids to go do something that they love doing and you hate doing, like going to the wacky pizza place with the automaton animals that play the piano. That will be a good way to spend your time.

Wouldn't it be great if your kids ran away? Then you wouldn't have to take care of their sorry asses anymore.

Here's what you should always say to your kids when they leave the house: "Good riddance."

Seven things you can
tell your kids to get
them to run away

❧ *I don't love you anymore.*

❧ *I doubt you're really mine anyway.*

❧ *Bus stations, train depots and homeless shelters have candy hidden in them. You just have to keep looking.*

❧ *Street hustling is a tried-and-true stepping-stone to movie stardom.*

❧ *Freight trains can take you anywhere.*

❧ *There are a lot of offers of free cigarettes out there in the world.*

❧ *A very small percentage of abductees are actually killed.*

The really bad thing about your kids is that they're just like you.

Stop and think about why you're doing all this for your kids. Basically, it's so they can grow up and have kids of their own. It's an unforgiving, ridiculous cycle. What's the point?

Your kids are ugly.

I know it's scary to admit, but sometimes you wish the law permitted you to kill your own kids.

You like one of your kids better than the others. And as much as you try to hide this, they all know the score.

You are an ATM machine, a bus driver, a landlord that offers free rent, a cook, a cleaning lady, and a nurse. But first and foremost, you are a chump.

You know those little school plays that you love to go see your kids in?
They suck.

Be sure to lie to your kids about the benevolent, all-seeing Santa Claus. It will prepare them for an adulthood of believing in God.

Would it be so bad if your kids found your gun and started playing with it?

You love your little tax deductions, don't you?

Lonely? Have kids. They'll be like an Alzheimer's patient at first, then they'll be like a high-maintenance pet, then they'll be like your worst enemy, then they might call once in a while. Finally, in your old age, they'll neglect you. By the way, this whole de-lonlification process will cost you a few hundred thousand dollars.

They say that since you need a license to fish, you should need a license to be a parent. I have a better idea. Let's just club all the babies that are born.

Your kids are ashamed of you.

When you're older and need your children's support, they will only give it begrudgingly.

Your kids laugh at you behind your back.

Think about your kids for a moment. They are a real disappointment to you, aren't they?

Your kids are even dumber than you.

"I created you in order to pass on my genetic code, but right now I'd settle for you just fetching me another beer."

Parenting is a wonderful and fulfilling blah blah blah. Face it, you're a glorified baby-sitter. And you don't even get paid.

If you want your family lineage to continue, why not have children with several partners. From a strictly evolutionary way of thinking, your chances of successful progeny would be much greater.

When your kids talk, pretend to be really interested. Keep up this charade for as long as they live.

"mommy! Look at me! Look! Mom! Look at me! Mom!!"

"uh-huh. Yeah. I see you."

You should really start worrying
when your kids start having sex.
Because that's just fucked up—
your kids having sex!

Your kids will grow up to be
just as screwed up as you.

Your kids are nothing special.
They're just like everybody else's kids.

When God gave you the precious gift of children, it was His way of totally fucking up your life.

Your kids go through your stuff when you're not home.

Your kids steal from you.

Your kids are embarrassed to be seen with you.

Why did you ever have to have these
rotten kids?

You have wasted the best years of your life on your kids.

You fancy yourself a pretty smart person. But consider this: Biology outsmarted you. Because despite all logic, it tricked you into believing it was a good idea to have kids.

Consider selling your children.

Your Annoying Pets

The only reason your pet sticks around is because you feed it.

If your cat were just a little bit bigger, it would kill and eat you.

Here's how your cat would kill you: It would wait for you to make a move, like running for your life, then it would pounce on you and inflict a mortal wound with its sharp teeth and powerful jaws. You would try to get up and run again, this time with blood streaming from your neck, your stomach, or wherever. Then your precious pet would bat at you several times and knock you down, inflicting more wounds with its massive claws. When you're white with blood loss and screaming for your neighbors or anyone within earshot to call an ambulance, your cat would grab your entire body in its mouth and shake you, perhaps gnawing your body in half. It would begin to eat your viscera while the top half of your body looked on in horror.

In the wild, your dog would eat you to survive.

Your pets don't really love you. They really just
want to escape from you.

If you have a cat in your house, that means you
also have a box of shit in your house.

If you have a dog, that means you have to
follow your dog around with a plastic bag and
scoop up its steaming feces with your bare hands.

You are enslaving your pet in your home.

Your pet is not your friend.
It is your hostage.

If your pet could talk, it would say, "Please, don't hurt me. What are your demands?"

The only difference between your house and a zoo is that you don't charge admission to the public to come and look at your pets and laugh at them.

Just stop and think how many times you've said "Shut up!" to your pet.

If times were tough, at least you could eat your pet.

*Admit it, when your pet has a serious ailment
and the vet tells you how much it will cost
to operate, you start wondering if your pet
is worth it.*

Why I hate cats:

- ❣ Cats scratch everything.

- ❣ Cats barf on everything.

- ❣ Cats shed hair on everything.

- ❣ Cats just want to be pet all the time. What am I, a full-time masseuse?

- ❣ Cats yowl all the time.

- ❣ Cats lick their own butts right in front of me while I'm trying to eat.

🐱 *Cats think they're better than me.*

🐱 *Cats are stuck-up.*

🐱 *Cats are mean.*

🐱 *Cats don't care if there are intruders in my house.*

🐱 *Cats just scurry around like rats most of the time. If they had tails that looked like a rat's, I would pay someone to poison them.*

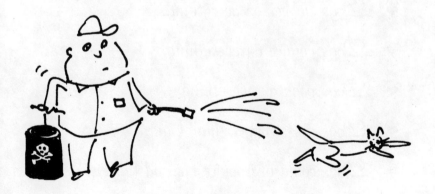

Why I hate dogs:

- Dogs lick everything.

- Dogs drool on everything.

- Dogs slobber on everything.

- Dogs pounce on everything.

- Dogs poop on everything.

- Dogs are stronger than I am.

- Dogs could overpower me and kill me.

- Dogs are too outgoing.

- 🐾 *Dogs give me the creeps.*

- 🐾 *Dogs are like big, dumb buddies who never leave. They're like Lenny from* Of Mice and Men, *only with deadly fangs and no bowel control.*

- 🐾 *Dogs are whiners.*

- 🐾 *Dogs are too damned happy all the time.*

- 🐾 *Dogs are too damned loud.*

- 🐾 *Dogs stink.*

"what is that god-awful smell?
oh, geez, it's the dog."

You probably have a pet just so you can feel like the master of something.

You allow a filthy, smelly animal free reign of your house. Who, I ask you, is the real master?

If your pet were just a few notches over on the species tree, you would kill it.

Your pets are incredibly stupid.

You are even more stupid than your pet, because you spend time and money feeding, housing, bathing, and otherwise tending to it, yet your pet just sits around all day and gets fat.

In your pet's universe, you are called "the ape that brings food."

When you talk to your pet like it's a baby, everybody wants to wring your neck.

That special bond you think you have with your pet is imaginary. As long as it has food and water, you could get hit by a train tomorrow, and your pet wouldn't think anything of it.

Are you one of those total loon-balls
that has a pet bird? What the hell
are you thinking?

"Hi birdie! I'm a freakin'
nutcase! Can you say that?
My master is a freakin' nutcase!"

Birds are nothing but cold, prickly squawking and pooping machines. You might as well have a pet bat.

When your pet dies, you will seriously consider putting its body in a dumpster.

I Can't Write

I'm sick of talking about you. I'd like to take a moment to unload a few of my own problems.

What do you think, I'm perfect? Just because I'm a counselor and I write self-help books doesn't mean I'm any less screwed up than you.

I really hate my writing. You probably do too. Don't even try to say something nice about it, it won't matter. I know I'm awful. I read back some of my writing and it's just embarrassing. I can't imagine that it's helping anybody. I am a complete fraud.

Did I ever tell you about the time I turned a paper in to my English teacher, Mr. Selnik, in the fifth grade? Oh, it was horrible. It was the first week of school, and Mr. Selnik, as a way to sort of get to know all his students, I guess, assigned us, as our very first assignment, an essay describing ourselves.

Well I was pretty interested in myself. I swear I poured my heart into that essay. I managed to fill a whole page, which in fifth grade is not too shabby. And when I handed it in, I couldn't have felt more proud. I pretty much assumed mine would be the best essay in the class, by far—maybe even the best essay Mr. Selnik had ever seen in all his years of teaching. I imagined him using my essay as an example of how to write for years to come, so all future generations of fifth graders would know what great writing looked like, for they would have seen perfection. He would frame my essay and hang it on the wall of the classroom. And periodically, he would refer to it reverently during a lesson. He would read a short passage from it on occasion, pausing afterward, maybe removing his glasses to wipe away a tear. "Beautiful," he would say. "Simply beautiful."

Well, what I didn't know at the time was that Mr. Selnik was a prick.

He handed everybody's essays back with big fat F's on them, and he proceeded to tell us how we should consider this a big warning. He said the grade wouldn't count, but that he hoped it would scare some good habits into us. He said that from now on he would not tolerate any misspellings, poor punctuation, or sloppy presentation in any assignment, ever. And he said that every last one of these essays had been riddled with examples of just such inexcusable errors.

You can imagine, I was pretty disappointed.

But what a prick! He could have told us to write about anything for this assignment, and imagine the gall of that guy to tell us to write something so personal, so close to home. "Describe yourself." He made us put our delicate eleven-year-old self-esteems right out there in the most vulnerable possible way, just so he could crush them. Of course, part of the sting of his evil lesson was that it would hit so close to the heart that we would likely never forget it. But looking back, I say it was just plain mean.

Well, as he was going off about how unacceptable these essays were, he grabbed one from the pile to use as an example of what he was talking about. You guessed it. It was mine. He went through every line, every word, pointing out every undotted *i*, every missing comma, every misspelling. I remember his ratchety, cigarette-worn voice vividly, dripping with bile and ridicule, "And look at this sentence: 'Besides my parents, I have a dog and two sisters and two fishies and I love them all very much.'" Then he sneered at the class and said, "That is a run-on sentence! The person who wrote this is a bad writer!"

I slumped in my seat, my freckled face as red as a baboon's ass. But he didn't stop there.

"This maudlin, self-indulgent nonsense has no place in a classroom in which the art of writing is practiced," he said, pacing down the rows of desks. Then he read on, mockingly, "'My friends,' spelled f-r-*e*-*i*-n-d-s, 'say that I am very fun to be around. My favorite color is blue. My name is Oswald and it comes from my grandfather, whose,'—spelled *w-h-o*-apostrophe-*s*,—'name was also Oswald,'" With this he looked right at me, and the entire class burst out laughing.

Boy, I just wanted to disappear, but he wouldn't let me. He stood over my desk for the next thirty-five minutes and read my entire essay out loud, pausing to point out every error, no matter how small. And when he was done, he said, "This doesn't sound like a very interesting person, does it? You see," he lectured, "bad writing reflects badly on the writer. You are what you write. And this person is a bad writer. Furthermore, judging by the bumbling, overemotive, and rather simplistic prose before me, I would also surmise that this writer is a sloppy, boring, unattractive person who is not very fun to be around."

Then, he dragged me by my ear to the front of the class and had me stand there while he ridiculed me openly—everything about me—my clothes, my hair, my teeth—you name it. I was sobbing like an infant. Of course, the class was eating it up. It was like a medieval roast.

Then he invited in a series of special guests: my parents, my sisters, my best friend, even my grandmother, whom he had had specially flown in from upstate New York at his own expense. He made them tell the class that everything I had written in my essay was a lie, that none of them loved me, or even knew me.

Then he pulled down my pants and urged all the other kids to laugh at how small and underdeveloped my penis was. He told them to throw things at me and taunt me, and they gleefully obliged.

He suggested that everyone tie me down and devour my genitals, but I don't think anyone heard him over the din of the mob.

For the rest of the year he never referred to me by name. He referred to me as "the bad writer."

So, every time I try to write a book I'm overcome with the visage of Mr. Selnik sneering at the entire class, holding up my story as an example of the very worst writing possible, and I have absolutely no confidence. Can you blame me?

Do you think you could help me? Would you write to me and tell me that my writing is good? I'd really appreciate it. I mean, come on, I'm trying to give you some helpful counseling in this book, and I don't think it's too much to ask to get a little back. I'm really putting myself out on the line here. All I'm asking for is a little sympathy, for Christ's sake.

And Mr. Selnik, if you're out there, if you haven't died yet, a letter from you would be especially nice. But if you still hate my writing, please don't write in to tell me so. God, I'd be crushed by that. Anyway, I hope you're dead.

You are a wage slave.

You would like to think you're hardworking, but let's face it: Two or three hours after you get up in the morning, you're ready to pack it in.

Ever have a really great idea, like for a little invention or something, then never do anything about it except maybe, at most, tell one of your friends? Then, a few months later, have you seen this very invention on the shelf in a store? You probably feel like you've had this experience, because it makes you feel like you have the potential to come up with great ideas, but actually, this has never happened to you.

You have no good ideas.

Listen to that little voice inside that says, "I don't have what it takes to do this job."

Perhaps if you wear shiny shoes to work, no one will notice that you're an incompetent loser.

All your hard work is just a cog in a machine. The purpose of that machine is to make someone you dislike very, very rich.

"Put a little more back muscle into it, Phipps."

They're paying you as little as they can get away with.

You don't deserve a penny more.

You should hang up on your cubicle wall precious pictures that your kids drew to prove that, at the very least, you can procreate.

Make sure you have a very amusing screen saver on your computer so everyone at work will know you are a keen arbiter of amusement.

Clip out cartoons from the newspaper comics page and hang them on your cubicle wall. These mediocre chuckle-getters will become lone rays of joy in your otherwise dreary existence.

"see, it's a funny cartoon about a pathetic guy who sits in a cubicle all day. Heh. Heh-heh. Heh. Heh. Heh-heh."

You are not creative.

When you laugh at work, you're really crying.
Think about it.

You are not contributing to the betterment
of humanity. In fact, you are a harbinger
of the apocalypse.

They could easily replace you.

You are not very smart.

The special skills you possess that help you perform your job could easily be taught to a zoo-monkey.

What purpose do you serve, exactly?

Why are you here?

You are not helping.

Go carry a file somewhere or something. But whatever you do, stay clear of the important stuff.

They should take you off the health plan.

*You haul your ass out of bed
and into the office every morning,
and for what?*

"I'm fired up to go help make
my boss even more rich today."

You hate your job. And it's safe to say no one at your job is particularly fond of you either.

If your workplace was somehow transplanted into the jungle and everyone was forced to survive at a very primitive level, it's safe to say that eventually your boss would rape you.

Someday your boss is going to call you into his office and explain why you have to be fired. Here's how it's going to go: He will say, "As you know, there have been some budget cuts, and we've had to make some very difficult decisions." Then you'll start crying and begging for your job. You'll look pathetic as you try to argue for your own worth. You won't change his mind. But he'll sit and let you yammer on, just because he feels like he has to. Really, he's just dying to get you out of there.

Your boss resents having to pay you.

You will never find a better job.

You don't deserve a raise. Here are eight reasons why:

1. You're getting paid too much already.

2. You'll never ask for one, because you're not the go-get-'em type.

3. You're a screwup.

4. That other guy you work with—the really sharp one—has much more promise. Basically, with him around, you don't stand a chance.

5. *You* have one fancy outfit that you wear periodically. Well, you think it's fancy, but really it's a damned eyesore. If they paid you more money, chances are you'd just blow it on more outfits like that, and nobody wants to see that happen.

6. *The* company can barely carry your deadweight as it is.

7. *You* do a half-assed job, so what they should really do is cut your pay in half.

8. *They're* thinking of firing you anyway.

Shut up and go back to your cubicle.

You need to be supervised.

You cannot be trusted to do your job
competently, so let's hire a middle manager to step
in after you've done your job and undermine all
your decisions, question your judgment, and
destroy your morale.

Someone should check on your work.

You do not deserve a window.

Who said you could have a plant in here?

Perhaps a security camera
mounted on your ceiling
would keep you on your toes.

Let's get you a smaller office.

The job you have now, is it the one you always dreamed of having?

*I would recommend
that you drown your sorrows
with a few drinks after work.*

"I hate my stupid job."

Maybe you should have a few drinks after work every day.

Develop a drinking problem.

You know that feeling when you show up at work first thing in the morning and your eyes are heavy—not only from being tired but also from crying about how meaningless your life is and how much you hate your job—and you don't want to be there today, and you feel uncomfortable in your dress-up clothes, and the taste of coffee is heavy in your mouth, and you wonder what the hell you're doing with your life? Get used to that feeling. You will feel it every day for the rest of your life.

There are certain tried-and-true techniques you can use to take control of your life, get the job you want, get the pay you deserve, and have a very satisfying, successful career. You will never learn these techniques.

You probably figure it's no big deal that you hate your job. Heck, the only reason you're there is to get a check so you can spend time with your family, because that's all that really matters in life. Trouble is, you hate your family, too.

Your ideas mean nothing.
Your supervisor will tell you the way
things ought to be.

"Just keep your stupid mouth shut and let me do the thinking.

Your boss has the gall to suspect you of stealing candy, spare change, and some other shit from the break room. And let's face it, you did steal that shit.

You are small-time.

You don't know what the hell you're doing.

Don't try anything bold or innovative. It will never work.

Break's over.

Go get me some coffee.

You are destined for mediocrity.

Your life is a blueprint for failure.

Why don't you make yourself useful and go make some copies of your ass.

Your Faith: What Has It Ever Brought You But Grief?

If there was a god who was all-powerful, all-knowing and all-seeing, he wouldn't give a rat's ass about you.

If there was a god, he wouldn't care how nice you dress when you go to church. In fact, he'd probably prefer that you go naked.

When you pray, no one is listening. Furthermore, you look ridiculous.

You'd better cake on the makeup and pour on the perfume for church, old ladies. You want the Lord to think you're hot, hot, hot.

Jesus was a dirty hippy.

Attention, Christians: In the Gospel According to Luke, Jesus promises his followers that he will return from the dead during their lifetimes and bring God's kingdom to Earth. He's running a little late. But keep waiting, he's sure to come any day now.

The pope isn't anything special. He's just a guy whose hat is bigger than anyone else's.

The religion you belong to is really just a cult, only bigger.

In the history of the world, more people have been killed because of religion than for any other reason.

God never makes mistakes. You can support almost any proposition with a quote from the Bible. But wait, a directly contradictory quote can always be found in a different part of the Bible. I guess God makes a shitload of mistakes.

God made a mistake when He made you.

I respect your right to hold your religious beliefs, and if they help you, I think that's great. I would, however, just like to inform you that you are a raving kook.

That book that came out a while ago about the secret code of numbers in the Bible proved to a lot of people that the Bible was foretelling future events. All of those people are kooks.

The president of the United States has religious-kook advisers.

There are people today who believe every word in the Bible as if it were literal truth, such as that the earth is fourteen thousand years old and was created in seven days. Many of those people have been elected to school boards.

God is your imaginary friend.

Every time someone says, "Thank you, God, for answering my prayer," there are a lot more people saying, "God, where were you when I needed you?"

When the chips are down, and you really need God's help, He's not going to be there for you, because He doesn't exist. But hey, maybe Santa will show up.

Here's what happens when you die: The blood stops flowing into your brain, and you have a few, last flickering thoughts, then you stop thinking altogether. The synapses in your brain stop firing, and your personality and thoughts cease to exist. Then your body decays. Grubs and boll weevils burrow into your head. Worms crawl in and out of your eye sockets. Maggots feed on your brain. Oh, wait. I'm getting it all wrong. Actually, you go to a country club–type place and hang out with Jesus, Mark Twain, and all your long-lost relatives. What was I thinking?

There's no such thing as a soul.

If you're thinking that you'll be reunited with
your dead loved ones someday, think again.
They're dead.

Buddhists believe in a circle of life in which you
are continually reborn until you break the circle
and reach Nirvana. They are all kooks.

Muslims believe you should kill a bunch of people in a holy war so you can get in Allah's good graces. Kooks.

Hindus are kooks, too.

Christians believe God, in His almighty wisdom, sent His only begotten son, Jesus Christ, born of a virgin, to die on the cross. Kooks.

Amish are fucking retards.

✍

If it weren't for science, the pope would probably still be torturing people who thought the earth revolved around the sun.

✍

If you're a Buddhist, and you think that after you die you're coming back to life as a higher being, I've got news for you: The only thing you're coming back as is maggot food.

*You do not have a personal relationship
with the Lord.*

"Oh, man, I'd love to hang out and be
your friend, but I've been dead for
2000 years. Sorry."

If there's a heaven like they say there is in the Bible, it'll be really boring. After just a few centuries—let alone an eternity—of doing nothing but sitting on a cloud and playing a harp, I promise you, you'll be ready to shove that harp right up somebody's ass.

A lot of people say that in a time of great trial or tragedy, their faith is all they had going for them. Faith in what? Jesus? God? If these guys are so great, why didn't they show up personally to help out? That's like a good friend saying, "Yeah, I know you're trapped in a well and you broke your leg. I'd come and save you, but I think I'm going to stay home and watch some TV—try to get by on just your faith in me."

God has forsaken you.

God wasn't the only one who forsook you in your
time of need. Buddha didn't show up. Neither
did the Virgin Mary, the Dalai Lama, Zeus,
or any of those guys.

Jesus doesn't really love you. He just loves the
way he feels when you're around.

God really seems to get off on all that
worshiping. That's gotta make you wonder.

Turn to the Bible for inspiration if you want, because it's supposed to be the divinely inspired word of God. But it strikes me as odd that Shakespeare, a mere mortal, was so much better, in terms of basic writing skill.

"Thine... Thy... Aw, crap. Get the dictionary. I always forget which is the plural possessive pronoun."

Why don't you make up your own religion? There's a lot of really funny combinations that no one's used yet.

Go ahead and have all the faith you want in your dullard superstitions. In the end, you'll be just as miserable as everybody else.

If you've got such a high regard for your religious faith, would you mind telling me why your life is still totally screwed up?

Why do those women on the religious-kook TV network have to wear so much hair spray? Are they attempting to fashion some kind of hair antennae to increase the strength of their signal up to heaven? That's my theory.

Maybe you should take a moment to be thankful for everything God has given to you: like all your misery, heartbreak, personal loss, and impending death.

Some prayer ideas

"God in heaven, I know you're completely make-believe and everything, but please let everyone around me think that I am somehow more pious than them. Thank you, and amen."

"Please, Easter Bunny, bring me plenty of eggs this year. And if you see Jesus, tell him we've been waiting for two thousand years for him to come back, and we're wondering if maybe he lost track of time."

"whatever you do, Lord, please don't ignore my prayers like you always do. Not this time. please... Please...? " Hello...?"

"Oh, Lord, grant me the serenity to accept the fact that you are a figment of my imagination, the courage to face my miserable life without pretending you're somehow there for me, and the wisdom to stop hanging up stupid prayer placards in my kitchen."

"Lord Jesus, I'm really curious. Were you gay? I mean, what was the deal with all that pacifism and hanging out with other men and never getting married? Not that I mind, but a lot of people would have a fit."

"Dear God, your most visible representatives here on Earth are all a bunch of kooks. Sorry."

"Dearest Poseidon, please protect me from great floods."

"*Dear Satan, hey, how's it going? You know, Jesus, God, the Holy Ghost, and all those guys have been bad-mouthing you something fierce.*"

"*Dear God, I understand that if I fail to believe in you, I'll burn in hell for all eternity. Thanks for being such a good sport about it.*"

Life: What's The Use?

A lot of my patients have asked why I don't just tell them to kill themselves.

Well, that's a good question.

I mean, I'll be honest with you, most of the sad sacks I offer counseling to would be better off dead. There was the guy who lost everything to his gambling addiction. He was a nice guy, and he meant well, but he kept throwing his money away at the track. His wife and kids eventually abandoned him, his parents stopped helping him pay his debts. He lost his job, the whole nine yards. And then he started getting chased by some, shall we say, "less than reputable" loan officers. He came into my office sweating and quivering, telling me that if he didn't come up with $10,000 fast, he was going to get his legs broken. I told him, "Buddy, your best option is to turn on the gas and stick your head in the oven." He looked at me like I was nuts, but come on—did he have a better option?

Oh, then there was this one lady who had cancer. God, that was hilarious. I mean, don't get me wrong, cancer is a very serious matter and I certainly do not mean to make light of it or belittle it in any way, but this lady *deserved* to die of cancer. Her singsongy whining reminded me of those funny "whiner" characters that used to be on TV. Remember them? They were a hoot. This lady was full of "my breast" this and "my self-image" that. I prit-near burst out laughing a couple times when she was pouring her heart out. Jesus Christ, lady, give it a rest. If life is that much of a struggle for you, maybe you should just give up the fight. She was really fat, too, which made her whole situation even funnier.

Sometimes suicide is the best way out. The company line in my field has always been, "Oh, it's a cry for help." Well, take it from me, that's a load of horseshit. Help? I'm telling you, sometimes you're beyond help. Sometimes the last thing you need is somebody to intervene and string you along for a few more miserable weeks with a few easy-to-swallow lies. Sometimes it's a really good idea to pack it in. And for some of these losers, coming up with a good idea is a big achievement. "Why not quit while you're ahead," I always tell them.

I've thought about taking my own life. Plenty of times. I even tried once. It's a really pathetic story.

I was about ten years old. I had pretty much figured out by then that life wasn't worth living. So I shut myself in my room and held my breath as long as I could. I figured this would cause me to die, since people who die don't breathe. Well, after a minute or so I couldn't hold it in anymore, and I let it all out. Then I *really* felt like a loser. I can't even kill myself right, I thought.

And, you know, in retrospect, I should say that I think that the true tragedy of suicide is the failed ones. Nothing is more pathetic than when you realize nothing's going your way, decide to kill yourself, then even that doesn't go your way.

Did you ever stop to think just how insignificant you are in the grand scheme of things? I mean, it doesn't really make any difference whether you live or die, does it?

The world would have been no different if you had never been born.

If only you had been aborted.

Suicide is a good idea. Because even if you slit your wrists and fail, you'll be left with a good conversation-starter right there on your forearms.

Suicide is a great way to send the message to your friends and family that you need help.

End your life now, and you'll be doing your part to decrease the greenhouse effect. And overpopulation. It's actually a pretty socially responsible thing to do, killing yourself.

Here's a great idea: Sit down in a comfortable place and begin to breathe very deeply. Be sure to inhale through your nose and exhale through your mouth. Now, shoot yourself in the head.

There's so much shit to do. But really, why bother with any of it? You're going to die eventually. Then you're really going to wonder why you bothered with all that shit.

There's a billion trillion galaxies in the universe. There's a billion trillion stars in our galaxy. There's a billion trillion planets circling those stars. You are just one of a billion trillion lifeforms on one of those planets. Would it really matter if you slit your wrists?

Would it really matter if you killed someone else?

The earth will probably get hit by a
big asteroid in the next few years,
and everyone who's in the path of that
asteroid will die instantly. Everyone else
will die a few months later from starvation
or radiation or marauding cannibals.
End your life now, while you can.

So, your life is really screwed up. That much we can agree on. But just pause and think for a second about how much work it would take to put your life back together. Think of all that struggle. I'm telling you, it's just not worth it.

Think about the sweet release of death.

You have a powerful self-preservation instinct. Everyone does. You must learn to ignore it and put yourself out of your misery.

If you're a famous rock star, a suicide
could be a good career move.

Since you're not a famous rock star,
not too many people would really care if you
died anyway, would they?

When you kill yourself, be sure to spray
the bullets around a bit and take some
other people with you.

When you kill yourself, you're going to
poop your pants. Oftentimes, this is the smell
that first alerts authorities to the bodies.
So, be courteous and go to the
bathroom beforehand.

Remember the Cold War? Remember for about fifty years people were scared of nuclear winter, fallout, and all that? I don't know why they're not scared anymore, because those nuclear weapons are still around. In fact, they're for sale to the highest bidder.

The people you know will get over your death soon enough.

It will only hurt for a second.

Actually, the carbon monoxide method doesn't hurt at all, I've heard.

Hopeless Role Models From History

"*I hate myself, my stupid friends, and every other fucking idiot on this godforsaken planet.*"
—**Benjamin Franklin**

"*Never before has anyone been more pathetic than me.*"
—**Winston Churchill**

"*The only thing I'm good at is losing. I'm worthless.*"
—**Abraham Lincoln**

"*Who among you even gives a rat's ass about me?*"

—Jesus Christ

"*No one finds me very attractive.*"

—Mohandas Gandhi

"*Who cares about my stupid dream anyway?*"

—Martin Luther King Jr.

"I just wish someone would show me some appreciation."
—**Michael Jordan**

"I don't have a single friend. Not one."
—**Ronald Reagan**

"I give up."
—**Helen Keller**

"I will never find someone who cares about me."
—**Adolf Hitler**

Epilogue

I'm really sorry I wrote this book. You didn't get anything out of it, I'm sure. And, basically, I just wasted your time and mine.

Now that I'm done writing it, I think I'm going to go out and buy a huge tub of ice cream and maybe some of those Keebler fudge-stripe cookies and I'm just going to sit in my bed and sob uncontrollably and eat that crap until I feel sick. I'll probably cry myself to sleep. Maybe I'll feel better in the morning.

Oh, God, and I just realized I have to go to work in the morning. I can't deal with sitting there and listening to people whine about their lives. Why do I even bother? I think I'll call in sick. I can't help those fuckups anyway. They're better off without me. I should just quit. I never wanted to be a psychologist anyway. I don't know what I want to be. I wish I could just end it all, but I don't have the guts.

I'm worthless.

And so are you.

Depress Yourself Every Day!

Order Dr. Pratt's Self-Hurt Cassette Series.

Hear Dr. Pratt's Daily Affirmation:

"You're worthless. Nobody likes you. You look terrible."

Learn . . .

the 3 steps to giving up hope.

the 7 attributes of a complete loser—how do you measure up?

And lots more!